# Walking with Ghosts

Qwo-Li Driskill is a Cherokee Two-Spirit/Queer writer and activist
also of African, Irish, Lenape, Lumbee, and Osage ascent. Hir work has
been included in *Shenandoah*, *Many Mountains Moving*, and in the
anthologies *Revolutionary Voices: A Multicultural Queer Youth Anthology* and
*Speak to Me Words: Essays on Contemporary American Indian Poetry*. S/he is
currently living in Three Fires (Ojibwe, Odawa, Potawatomi) and Huron
territories while pursuing a PhD in Rhetoric and Writing at Michigan
State University.

**Earthworks Series**
*Series Editor:* Janet McAdams

# Walking with Ghosts

Qwo-Li Driskill

SALT

CAMBRIDGE

PUBLISHED BY SALT PUBLISHING
PO Box 937, Great Wilbraham, Cambridge PDO CB1 5JX United Kingdom

First published 2005

Printed and bound in the United Kingdom by Lightning Source

Typeset in Swift 9.5 / 13

ISBN 1 84471 113 7 paperback

SP

1 3 5 7 9 8 6 4 2

*For those who survived*

# Contents

# Acknowledgments

Some of the poems in Walking with Ghosts originally appeared or are forthcoming in the following publications:

*Bloom*; *Crab Orchard Review*; *Confluere*.com; *ColorsNW Magazine*; *The Crucible*; *Evergreen Chronicles: A Journal of Gay, Lesbian, Bisexual and Transgender Arts and Culture*; *Lodestar Quarterly*; *Many Mountains Moving: A Literary Journal of Diverse Contemporary Voices*; *News from Nowhere*; *Poetsagainstthewar*.org; *The Raven Chronicles*; *Red Ink Magazine*; *Revolutionary Voices: A Multicultural Queer Youth Anthology*; *Shenandoah: The Washington & Lee University Review*; *Stepping Out*; *Sky Woman Falls into the New Millennium*; *XCP: Streetnotes*.

Wa'do to all of my ancestors.

Wa'do to the Cheyenne, Duwamish, Huron, Ojibwe, Odawa, and Potawatomi Nations, on whose lands I wrote these poems.

Wa'do to my parents, Paul and Jeannie Driskill, for their love and support.

Wa'do to the rest of my family: Dylan, Taylor, Rachel, Rebecca, Kayla, Mary Kay, and Kim.

Wa'do to Colin Kennedy Donovan, for hir friendship over the last two decades. Gvgeyu, ahwin.

Wa'do to all the folks who have given me love, support, hope, and have helped me through the process of creating and revising these poems: the students at American Indian Heritage Middle College, Boo Balkan, Ahimsa Timoteo Bodhrán, Jen Boland, Jenn Bowman, Martha Brice, Gabi Clayton, Mary Lee Colby, Sasha Summer Cousineau, Ellen Cushman, Louis Esmé Cruz, Samonte Cruz, Candiss Eickelmann, Marcus Embry, Laurie Lynn Hogan, Craig Hymson, Betsy Geist, Bruce Gordon, Janice Gould, Angela Haas, seth hannah, Daniel Heath Justice, the folks at the Kenyon Review 2003 Writers Workshop, Uchechi Kalu, Rita Brady Kiefer, Ben Lallátin, Kim Lee, Vicki Lopez, Ann McCormick, Deborah Miranda, Dani Montgomery, Erik Nagler, Ami Peters, Pamela Porter, Pauline Mitchell, Malea Powell, william maria rain, Rebecca Sandel, Arlo Starr, Marcus Strash, Amy Sonnie, basiL shadid, Tsi-ge'-yu Sharp, Rae Thomas, Noah B. West, and Marie-Elise Wheatwind. Wa'do to Janet McAdams for her work as an editor on this manuscript and this series. Wa'do to anyone I may have forgotten to list here. Wa'do, y'all. This book could not have been written without your loving-kindness.

# Tal'-s-go Gal'-quo-gi Di-del'-qua-s-do-di Tsa-la-gi Di-go-whe-li/ Beginning Cherokee

*I-gv-yi-i Tsa-la-gi Go-whe-lv-i: A-sgo-hni-ho-'i/*

## FIRST CHEROKEE LESSON: MOURNING

Find a flint blade
Use your teeth as a whetstone

Cut your hair
Talk to shadows and crows

Cry your red throat raw

Learn to translate the words you miss most:
*dust*               *love*                  *poetry*

Learn to say       *home*

My cracked earth lips
drip words not sung
as lullabies to my infant ears
not laughed over dinner
or choked on in despair
No

They played dead until
the soldiers passed
covered the fields like corpses
and escaped into the mountains
When it's safe we'll find you
they promised
But we were already gone
before sunrise

I crawl through a field of
twisted bodies to find them
I do everything Beginning Cherokee
tells me
Train my tongue
to lie still
Keep teeth tight
against lips
Listen to instruction tapes
Study flash cards

How can I greet my ancestors in a language they don't
        understand

My tear ducts fill with milk
because what I most love
was lost at birth

My blood roars skin to blisters
weeps haunted calls of owls
bones splinter
jut through skin
until all of me
is wounded
as this tongue

*Ta-li-ne-i Tsa-la-gi Go-whe-lv-i: A-ni-s-gi-li/*

SECOND CHEROKEE LESSON: GHOSTS

Leave your hair
at the foot of your bed

Scratch your tongue
with a cricket's claw to speak again

Stop the blood with cornmeal

Your ancestors will surround you as you sleep
keep away ghosts of generals presidents       priests
who hunger for your
rare and tender tongue

They will keep away ghosts
so you have strength
to battle the living

Stories float through lives
with an owl's sudden swooping
*I knew some Cherokee*
*when I was little*
*My cousins taught me*
My mother watches it all happen again
sees ghosts rush at our throats
with talons drawn like bayonets
*When I came home speaking*
*your grandmother told me*

I forbid you to speak that language
in my house
Learn something useful

We sit at the kitchen table
As she drinks iced tea
in the middle of winter
I teach her to say *u-ga-lo-ga-go-tlv-tv-nv/* tea
across plastic buckets of generic peanut butter
wonder bread diet coke
Try to teach her something useful

I am haunted by loss
My stomach is a knot of serpents
and my hair grows out
as owl feathers

*Tso-i-ne-i Tsa-la-gi Go-whe-lv-i: A-nv-da-di-s-di |*

## THIRD CHEROKEE LESSON: MEMORY

Raid archeologists' camps
and steal shovels
to rebury the dead

Gather stories like harvest
and sing honor songs

Save the seeds
to carry you through the winter

Bury them deep in your flesh

Weep into your palms
until stories take root
in your bones
split skin
blossom

There are stories caught
in my mother's hair
I can't bear the weight of

*Could you give me a braid*
*straight down the middle*
*of my back just the way I like*
So I part her black-going-silver hair
into three strands
thick as our history
radiant as crow wings

This is what it means to be Indian
Begging for stories in a living room
stacked high with newspapers magazines baby toys

*Mama story me*

She remembers
  Great Grandmother Nancy Harmon
  who heard white women
  call her uppity Indian during
  a quilting bee
  and climbed down their chimney with
  a knife between her teeth

She remembers
  flour sack dresses
  tar paper shacks
  dust storms  blood  escape

She carries fire on her back
My fingers work swiftly as spiders
and the words that beat in my throat
are dragonflies

She passes stories down to me
I pass words up to her
Braid her hair

It's what she doesn't say
that could destroy me
what she can't say
She weeps milk

*Nv-gi-ne-i Tsa-la-gi Go-whe-lv-i: U-de-nv/*

FOURTH CHEROKEE LESSON: BIRTH

> Gather riverbank clay
> to make a bowl
>
> Fill it with hot tears
>
> Strap it to your back
> with spider silk
>
> Keep your flint knife close
> to ward off death
> and slice through umbilical cords
>
> Be prepared for blood

Born without a womb
I wait for the crown of fire
the point where further stretching is impossible
This birth could split me
I nudge each syllable into movement
Memorize their smells
Listen to their strange sleepy sounds
They shriek with hunger and loss
I hold them to my chest and weep milk
My breasts are filled with tears

I wrap my hair around their small bodies
a river of owl feathers

*See* they whisper *We found you*
*We made a promise*

This time we'll be more careful
Not lose each other in
the chaos of slaughter

We are together at sunrise
from dust we sprout love and poetry
We are home
Greeting our ancestors
with rare and tender tongues

# Map of the Americas

I wish when we touch
we could transcend history in
double helixes of dark and light
on wings we build ourselves

But this land grows volcanic
with the smoldering hum of bones
All that's left
of men who watched beloveds
torn apart by rifles
Grandmothers singing back
lost families
Children who didn't live
long enough to cradle a lover
arms around waist
lips gently skimming nape
legs twined together
like a river cane basket

Sometimes I look at you
and choke back sobs knowing
you are here
because so many of my people
are not

Look:  my body curled and asleep
becomes a map of the Americas

My hair
spread upon          the pillow
   a landscape of ice  My chest the plains
      and hills of this land My spine
            the continental divide
            my heart drums the
            rhythm of returning
            buffalo herds Do you
         notice the deserts
               and green
                  mountains
                     on my belly's
                     topography
                     or the
                        way
                        my
                           hips
                              rise
                              like
                              ancient pyramids
                           My legs wrapped with the
                     Amazon the Andes the Pampas
                        the vast roads of the Incas
                              here are rainforests
                              highlands
                              stolen breath
                                 trapped deep
                                 in mine
                              shafts and
                                 my feet
                                    that reach
                                       to touch
                                          Antarctica

When your hands travel
across my hemispheres
know these lands
have been invaded before
and though I may quiver
from your touch
there is still a war

It is not without fear
and memories awash in blood
that I allow you to slip between
my borders
rest in the warm valleys
of my sovereign body
offer you feasts and songs
dress you in a cloak of peacock
feathers and stars
These gifts could be misconstrued
as worship
Honor mistaken for surrender

When you taste my lips
think of maize
venison
perfect wild strawberries

Notice the way my breath smells of cedar
my sweat flows like slow Southern rivers
and my flesh burns with history

Honor this

I walk out of genocide to touch you

# Going Home

*Never forget*
*America is our Hitler*

Chrystos

## New Echota, Georgia

We went back there
The air hot and thick as we
move across a field
that was once a street.

The city is a museum now.
Buildings burnt to the ground
by white farmers
are reconstructed:
the court with its stanch protestant benches,
a council house with only four white walls,
the *Cherokee Phoenix*
where Sequoyah's syllabary
printed leaf upon leaf.

In the courthouse, a small bird
crashes violently against a window.
I open my palms and she lands in them.
I take her outside.
*A spirit* my mother and I say.

We photograph
a small garden of corn,
an old dark cabin,
a missionary's house,
one of the detention camps
we were forced into.

Marked with a small plaque,
there's only grass and trees there, now,
and the soft sobs of grandmothers
that will never leave the earth.


HOPKINSVILLE, KENTUCKY

The Trail of Tears Commemorative Park
grieves next to the South Fork Little River.
On the edge of a vast parking lot
the graves of two chiefs moan.

On the other side of the river,
hundreds of ancestors unmarked.
*Children and elders,*
*for the most part*
my mother points out.

The center of the parking lot
displays flags of the states
the Trail was forced through.
I notice a small bird trapped
inside a lamp near the ground.

My father takes a screwdriver,
disassembles the lamp,
and lets her escape,
returning east.

SPRINGFIELD, MISSOURI

*Trail of Tears? Never heard of such a thing.*
*Wouldn't you like to see a Civil War Monument?*


TAHLEQUAH, OKLAHOMA

One thousand miles back home.


NEW ECHOTA, GEORGIA

We have no tobacco to feed our ancestors.
We move across fields and through woods.
My mother asks,
*Do you feel like we're walking with ghosts?*

We are, mama.

# For Arabs and Indians
## and Others who Love Cedars

After the egos of nations
subtract soil from earth
leave shallow trenches
muddied by blood

Arabs and Indians
and others who love cedars
remember how to read history in
red ochre curves of wood
and how roots weave ceremonies
push through the surface like arms
reaching for the disappeared

We know roots
thick as hair
wrap themselves around
femurs
      jaws
          wrists
pull witness into spiked leaves

Arabs and Indians lift sprigs of cedar
to their noses
inhale its scent
give thanks to the branch that gifts it
leave offerings in the shallow trenches left
after the egos of nations

Especially for william maria rain and basil shadid.

# Ghost Dances

Sagwu'i/ One

The white kids at the next table
gulp coffee with
too much sugar,
laugh at Mexican accents.

That one wears a backwards baseball cap.
A wide-eyed grinning Indian with feather
stares me down from blue fabric.

The white kids at the next table
act like they are supposed to be here.

If they die in a car crash,
I will know Wovoka pushed them.

Ta'li/ Two

A mixed-blood
Ghost Dances.
Which of my people come back?

Jo'i/ Three

When the soldiers come
to stop us from dancing,
will they kill me in quarters?

NVHGI/ FOUR

Does an Indian
drag queen
mouth the words
to a woman's mourning song?
Does an Indian
drag queen
Ghost Dance backwards?

HISGI/ FIVE

Balboa commanded his
*perros de guerra*
to rip the Two-Spirits into pieces.
In pieces, how do we dance?

SUDALI/ SIX

Robert Kennedy hit a tree on Aspen Mountain.
Wovoka planted it.

An airplane filled with Americans
crashes in the Atlantic ocean.
Wovoka dances on its wings.

Everywhere I look, I believe in the Ghost Dance.

GALIQUOGI/ SEVEN

*The AIDS Memorial Quilt in Washington, D.C.*
*October, 1996*

There are many ways to dance.
I walk backwards through a giant quilt of
names whispered into the hollows of our mouths.

One mile is no comfort,
a mass grave,
a long war.

And how can we ever
gather up all of our ghosts,
kiss each of them on the cheek
and say,

*Everything's gonna be all right.*
*It's time to go home now, sugar.*
*It's time to go home.*

# Love Poems for Billy Jack

I.

Let's laugh down
the Alabama sky
warm and moist as
mouths on cocks

Your soft rough elegance
moves against me
like flint over stone
molecules exploding on tongues

I could have kissed
your face
      pulverized by fists
legs
      splintered by ax handle
folded into you
like your living body
      in the trunk of your car

Loved you to your blue diamond
          white sapphire
        center

II.

Did these men, these boys
rest their eyes too long
on the curve of
your forearm

Did your salty musk
bring goose bumps
Did the way you ran hand through
hair make them catch their breath

Was it they noticed the hard
lines of men's hands
the way blue jeans hang
on men's waists

Were they afraid
of wanting you soft as
owl feathers brushing the stars
of Coosa County

These men, these boys
who smashed your face unrecognizable
        mutilated sternum
                doused tires in gasoline
watched you as you became
        garish gold flame
                sun hot kindling
                        eye sockets
                        shot through with red plumes

wanted to hear you
    snap and spark like cedar

        black smoke banshee shrieking
          in the Alabama dark

III.

They could have loved you

Found your hands red hot on pectorals
Atomic tongue down spines

*(They needed you alive dancing flame)*

They could have written you love poems
    with diamond-sapphire
        centers

*(They needed you alive dancing flame)*

IV.

These words will lick
up your last breath

You too hot in bones man
You rough elegant ghost man
You once alive man
burn me
to sky

*In memoriam: Billy Jack Gaither*

## Summer Haiku

Been thinkin bout words
n the way yr hand
cups my belly like water

## To Your Rude Question, *What's Your Pedigree?*
## A Response

Grandmother planted the tree
Brother got lynched from
Daddy chopped it down

# High Yella Sonnet

Every mornin I pull plastic comb through thick
copperbrown curls, stare at a face
ancestors kissed n colored with a trick
of high yella light. My index finger trace

my body's cedar n ebony trails
to colonization's pale n puffy scars: a steel bit
in my mouth, shinin web of rails
construct to open my interior, rivers covered in grit

n oil. Look at my hybrid corn n sweet potato skin,
yella as gold stole from homelands.
My blood aint subterranean,
I bear pockmarks of forged treaties, iron brands.

You call me watered down, say my peoples good as dead.
I laugh n stand before you, fullblood high yella, black n red.

# Wild Indians

Yes you could say I am wild
I don't like flower gardens to be kept up
Don't like TV lies
and I would scalp you in a second

Yes I'm wild
I can't find God in white walled churches
Don't like the pope
and would scalp him in a blink

I'm wild
Don't like cages
Can't walk on a leash
and never eat the food you leave out

Wild as hell
means you better treasure that scalp of yours
cuz I've got some dancing to do
and that scalp might be just what I need

## What You Must Do

First, call the words from your marrow.
Pull them from strands of muscle,
dark and warm.
You will bleed.
Form them into clay.
Breathe.

Then, offer them your flesh.
They will take nothing less.

Run with your words to the top of a cliff.
Let go.

Hurry.

They come for us in the morning.

# For Marsha P. (Pay It No Mind!) Johnson

*found floating in the Hudson River shortly after NYC Pride, 1992*

> *You are the one whose spirit is present in the dappled stars.*
> JOY HARJO *from "For Anna Mae Pictou Aquash..."*

Each act of war
is whispered from
Queen to Queen
held like a lost child
then released into the water below.
Names float into rivers
gentle blooms of African Violets.

I will be the one that dangles
from the side but
does not let go.

The police insisted you leapt
into the Hudson
    driftwood body
    in sequin lace
    rhinestone beads
    that pull us to the bottom.
Just another dead Queen.

I am the one who sings Billie Holiday
as a prayer song to you, Marsha P.

We choke on splintered bones,
dismembered screams,
the knowledge that each
death is our own.

I pour libations of dove's blood,
leave offerings of yam and corn
to call back all of our lost spirits.

Marsha P, your face glitters with
Ashanti gold
as you sashay across the moonscape
in a ruby chariot ablaze.
Sister, you drag
us behind you.

When we gather on the bridge between
survival and despair,
I will be the one wearing gardenias
in my hair,
thinking about
how we all go back to water.
Thinking about
the night
you did not jump.

I will be the one
with the rattlesnake that binds
my left arm and
in my right hand I will carry
a wooden hatchet to
cut away at the
silence of your murder,
to bite down hard on the steel of despair.

Girl, I will put your photo
on my ancestral altar
to remember all of us
who never jumped.

Miss Johnson, your meanings
sparkle like stars dappled
across the piers of the
Hudson River.

Gathered on the bridge
we resist the water.

# In Our Oldest Language

Tsuj'/ Boy, you are galvlo'/ sky
continually above me
I am eloh'/earth your hands reach
inside to aching molten rock
Your fingers gilded wings
that rise and thrust against
dark muscle rhythms
rock me until I am coiled
around you blooming

Your lightning tongue
summons me to skim
the sweltering expanse of your back
tempts me to nvyoi/ the rocky place
between your thighs where
you are hard as a cedar flute
asdaya/ taut
as a drum

Water swells at your bank
threatens to break loose
But I am slow
so slow
and steady as sparrows
Nibble and suck
strawberries
Flick my tongue across their dark tips
uwansv ale tsuwodu/ ripe and beautiful
Lure their flavor to the surface of your skin

My mouth hungry for your pulse
even and soft on my lips
My hands blanketed by your hair
Your chest silvered and wet
against mine

Vv/ Yes
Our moans a low fierce rumble
a coming storm

# Letter to Tsi-ge'-yu

Tonight your tears
follow me home
Hover around my shoulders
like a *ske'na*
haunting as history
bright and wondrous as fireflies

Tsi-ge'-yu
160 years ago
they rounded us up with guns
filled rivers with our blood
stripped our lives to marrow and
beat us with the bones

We are still trying to escape soldiers
hide our babies
hold on to clods of earth
as they drag us away by our feet
screaming and bloodied

*Our families are supposed*
*to tell us these stories*
you say
*You're my family now*

Tsi-ge'-yu
Tonight I pluck
your tears from air
wrap them in deerskin
string them on spider silk

Look
I wear them
around my neck like cornbeads

| *selu* | corn |
|--------|------|
| *giga* | blood |
| *sgilu:gi* | You are my sister |
| *gvhwanosda* | whole |

These are the words our bodies
were not meant to carry
but do

These survival songs
put us back together

In this city that
does not belong to us,
we sink our teeth deep into
words ripped from our mamas' mouths

| *tsuko:li* | bones |
|------------|-------|
| *kanoges:sdi* | history |

sink our teeth deep and
repeat what we know is sacred

**Cherokee Translations:**

*Tsi-ge'-yu*: "Beloved." Literally, "I love her/him."

*ske'na*: human or animal ghost

# For Matthew

*I have died too many deaths
that were not mine.*
AUDRE LORDE

I have found my body collapsible,
choking on your death
like a small child who seeks to understand
by stuffing pennies and marbles into mouth.

It reverberates across the continent,
fallout from an old, old story.
How when they found you,
at first they thought you were a scarecrow
crucified on a Wyoming fence.

In Seattle, 1000 lit candles.
(I wanted the city to burn.)

In San Francisco, a rainbow flag hung half-mast.
(I wanted earth to split open.)

In DC, the president finally spoke.
(I wanted screams to shatter glass.)

In Laramie, they wore armbands.
(I wanted a revolution.)

Thousands upon thousands say *Never Again, Never Again.*
(I don't want to remember you as *symbol.*)

We have no more time for symbols.
We have no more time for vigils.
We have no more time

because when I started writing
this poem for you, Matthew,

you were still *alive*.


*In memoriam: Matthew Shepard*

## The Leading Causes of Death
## Among American Indians

The first is heart disease,
followed by accidental death.

The original accident was Columbus
bumping into this place,

though everyone says he wasn't such a bad guy,
he just thought we'd make the perfect slaves.

That was an accident too, since we just died
of broken hearts, so white folks had to find

another group to enslave. Which reminds me,
Africans under apartheid had a whole lot of accidents.

How many staircases are there to fall down?
How many showers can we slip in?

My heart is not a give away.
My rage is not an honor song.

I am tired of all these accidents.
I am drunk on anger,

driving head on into a wall called America
praying one day

the leading cause of death among American Indians
will be that we are old.

# Snapshot

Tell me it isn't you in the photograph. Say
it's a 21st century trick or the poor quality
of newsprint. It was in this box, the picture
of you with your swaggering smile stand-
ing in front of the sandcastle we built.
Someone must have cut your head out of
that picture, pasted it here. No sandcastle
in the background; a stack of bodies. Not
turrets and spires; the sharp points of black
hoods. Your lips imprinted hope on the soft
underside of my heart. I named your right
hand Comfort, your left hand Strength.
Your face was safe harbor. An Iraqi man
howls, twists against a wall yellowed as
dogs' teeth. A soldier stares out at me,
grinning. Say it isn't you. Give me an
argument for absolution: enough to erode
blood. Say it isn't you. I can't bear looking.

# Eulogy for the 40th

*A city that is set on an hill cannot be hid.*
MATTHEW 5:16

I.

When I kiss my lover, a generation of ghosts rises like dust, like
    pale moths from his vibrant tongue, nests in my hair.

Today Reagan's body flies under armed guard for burial in
    California
near books decided upstanding enough to escape fires.

Close down Wall Street give the postal workers a day off shut the
    banks to remember life upon life upon life he gobbled up.

We're tired of the newspaper, TV, radio, mourning him.

We're tired of *Taps*.

We can't listen to one more remembrance from Thatcher or
    Dubya or his Mexican
chef during the 1983 G7 summit.

When I kiss my lover, a generation of ghosts rises like dust, like
    pale moths from his vibrant tongue.

We don't care if Ronnie was a gentleman or looked good in
    cowboy boots. Please, don't talk about the smile flashing
    in his eyes.

Murdered nuns flashed in his eyes. Granada, Nicaragua, El
    Salvador, AIDS flashed in his eyes.

King of Lies. Composer of Invasion. Leader of Genocide. Lover of
Blood.

Say it: we're not sad to see him go. No one I know shed a single
tear for his passing.

When I kiss my lover, a generation of ghosts rises.

II.

Say it: there's not a tear left to shed after
mourning our families lovers childhoods.
More to come. We all know it's true. A city
set on a hill cannot be hid. Go on, rewrite
history. Name him Father of Peace. Look:
The water makes you glow in the dark.
Air buries a tumor's seed in your throat.
Trickledown economics left you covered
in blood. Mass graves in Argentina. Mass
graves in Iraq. Mass graves in Guatemala.
Mass graves in (your name here.)

*Unnumbered.*

A city set
upon a hill
cannot
cannot
cannot
be hid.

> We sing from trenches.
> Foundations. Sewers.
> Abandoned mines sour with bones.
> Mud shrouds are only cocoons—
> unravel them into a single silk strand.
> Deceit's gray dust makes us fly.

III.

*Hardly anyone survived.*
My lover is a soldier from the front lines of despair.
*Everyone was dying.*

Sometimes he watches ghosts in the corner of the room,
tells me stories.
*Dead. Every single one of those men.*
*Dead.*

For eight years Reagan did nothing.
We died by the fistful, then by the thousands.
He handsomely drank Scotch with
the Bush family, famous smile flashing,
watching plans for his city on a hill take hold.

Look at us now.
AIDS is as casual as weather.
The Quilt is too large to be shown in a single location.
My generation is resented for not knowing life before.
The generation before us is resented for knowing.
We use words like *serodiscordant* and don't break down.
Overnight posters are plastered:
*1 in 7 Gay and Bi Men in Seattle is HIV+.*
When I kiss my lover ghosts rise.

Look at the war that flashes behind
his eyes. Look! Acres of unfurling dead.

I still want to believe
an army of lovers cannot lose.

IV.

June 12, 2004

Dear Ronald,

When I kiss my lover,
a generation rises.
My lips brush your wars
from his perfect face.

With my arm laced with his
let me press my cheek against the flag and weep,
watch them lower your mahogany casket.

Ronald,
Let me fill my fist with California dirt.
Let me be the first to say

*Goodbye.*

*Especially for Bruce*

## Grandmother Spider's Lesson for an Urban Indian Queer

She clings to her web, four stories up, holds fast against the Seattle wind and rain. Her abdomen is a perfect black bead that catches light like a crystal. Her legs delicate as an infant's hands. She weaves a night threaded with moonbeams. Grandmother is alive, four stories up. "Grandmother," I say, "we never stop spinning from one death to another, from one impossible situation to the next. This is a city where homeless Indians have their noses broken by skinheads, where Queer kids sell their bodies to eat tomorrow. We have no reflections here. They think we should be ghosts."

*Sugar*, she laughs, *just keep weaving. Don't let them tear you down. Look! I am alive, four stories up! They build sky scrapers on top of our homes, but we're still here.*

Her body is silhouetted against the Seattle skyline, miracle spider alive four stories up.

*Cling fast*, she tells me. *Keep weaving. Life will stick.*

ᎬᎬᏳ ᎥᏔᏥ ᏣᎳᏲ

ᎠᎦᎶᏳ
ᎠᏥᏣᎤᏍ ᎥᎤᎯ
ᏎᏣᏔ ᎥᎵ

GVGEYU' HAIKU TSALAGI

Aquadan'togi
atsilvsga hawini
ganhgo'i sali

CHEROKEE LOVE HAIKU

My embodied heart
blooms, opens beneath
his persimmon tongue.

## Gay Nigger Number One

*"Yonder they do not love your flesh. They despise it. They don't love your eyes, they'd just as soon pick em out. No more do they love the skin on your back. Yonder they flay it. And O my people they do not love your hands. Those they only use, tie, bind, chop off and leave empty. Love your hands! Love them. Raise them up and kiss them."*

Baby Suggs, *Beloved*. TONI MORRISON

In this season of blood
I try to harvest
life from your planted body

Spring cherry trees bloom
thousands of dove-white skulls
Branches rattle down loose teeth
The sun sorrow hot
as I carry your ghost
heavy in my arms

I am just a poet
my words brittle
against the mad butcher's knife
that cut away at your lips with
exact delicacy
skinning deep
violet plums

Your hands forever disappeared
Brown sweet pomegranate fingertips
stolen by that ghoul
your mother loved

All he left was
your skull bleached of color
scrawled with the words
Gay Nigger Number One

Too strange a fruit
for the cover of Time
the country collaborates
bleaches your name off the page

Steen last night
I heard your screams in
each drop of rain

If I were Isis
I would gather up your
hacked-to-bits body
weep you alive


*In memoriam: Steen Keith Fenrich*

# Lullaby

*I know*
*I love you*
*I believe you*
*You're safe now*

If I could I would slip backwards
Become a rattlesnake
with burning venom
coiled and ready to strike
before anyone could cut
you again

I pray for our ghosts
to make us whole
These tears are acid to burn
out horror
These words singe me
Dangerous dirges

If I could I would sing you a song
that would make daddy vanish
make momma stop
maybe hide you someplace
warm and safe
maybe teach you to fashion
weapons from rocks

I see you
a baby girl
pulling a new and proud walking self
to your mother
Her hand earthquakes you down
loud as thunder when lightning
splits the air near your skin

I am sweating ink
You speak words
you were never supposed to
Your tongue a shield

If I could I would rock you back home
Sing you the songs your mother forgot
Dance you a ceremony to return
each shard of bone pulled
from your muscles

If I could I would rock you to green

*I know*
*I love you*
*I believe you*
*You're safe now*

# What You Gave Me
*for Colin*

Words were trapped inside
You opened fingers
pulled scales from my shrunken tongue

# Allotment T'ang

| | | | | |
|---|---|---|---|---|
| chop | split | steal | land | take |
| sew | plot | farm | dust | rake |
| white | hate | chew | red | land |
| stomp | ground | pray | heart | break |

## On Hearing Another Friend Was Raped
*for D.G.*

Like a shawl of sorrow
I wrap your story around my shoulders
bless your bruises
as defiant gestures of skin

I wrap your story around my shoulders
let it tangle and knit with mine
as defiant gestures of skin
a complex network of roots

Let it tangle and knit with mine
your marked neck, my scratched heart
a complex network of roots
that sings the body to sacred ground

Your marked neck, my scratched heart
are wounds we permit to fall away
that sing the body into sacred ground
where we harvest blooming crops of resistance

Our wounds we permit to fall away
into the fertile soil of silence
where we harvest blooming crops of resistance
and pluck redemption from our scars

Into the fertile soil of silence
we return, stubborn and gorgeous
and pluck redemption from our scars
weave songs from the movement of spheres

We return, stubborn and gorgeous
Bless your bruises
weave songs from the movement of spheres
like a shawl of sorrow

# Love Poems: 1838–1839

## TENNESSEE

What was left behind?

    Love formulas
written in dark syllables,
whose incantations
    undulated
like our tongues.

(Did you know they tried to
erase you, forbade me to
speak your name?)

My arms, muscled rivers
you came to
each morning.

(After they seized you
they told me not to touch
anyone again.)

Rows of corn,
ears swaying slightly on
    their stalks;
pumpkins thick with flesh;
tomatoes swollen with juice,
    so acidic
they could blister your lips.

## INDIAN TERRITORY

I know you were driven away,
taken from everything that
    taught you love.

I don't expect you to forget,
only to love me as well.

Love me.

Love the winding trails to my
    belly,
the valleys at my sternum,
the way I slope towards you like
    promise.

Who comforted you
as you hugged knees to your
    bruised body?

Who laid you down, covered you
    with kisses
as you cried,
"My bones shriek like trains
filled with Nations!"

(Did you know when you left          Who held you as you convulsed,
they drank every drop?)              "My body is an open-mouthed
                                          moan!"

A quilt appliquéd with stars
so you could remember                Who gave your body
the birth of the Milky Way.          back to you?

(Or was it a map, coded,             Hush.
to find your way back to me?)
                                     This is home now.
What was left behind?

    Corn.                            You are home.
       Tongues.                      You are home.
    Scraps of stars. Words.
 And your body's
    silhouette
scratched forever into me.

## Evening With Andrew Jackson

Andrew Jackson walks down Eighth Avenue,
passes the Circle K,
walks all the way to Seventeenth Street
turns right
and knocks on my door.

He looks good for being
dead for so long, so I decide to let him in.
I figure he's taken everything,
so what do I have to lose?

His fingers open from
his rotting palm like gray dead trees.
He points back towards the street.

I walk out the door and see blood like satin ribbons
trailing across sidewalks, through lawns, and down the
highway he came here on.

Red lines flow from the sign at Mohawk Carpets,
trickle from bottles of Arizona Iced Tea chilled on gas station
      shelves
and curdle in the Land O Lakes Butter in the
dairy section of the grocery store.

I follow his trail
past a frat boy sleeping in a
Florida Seminole t-shirt,
past the Super Wal-Mart,
through the basement of
the First Presbyterian Church
where a two year old girl
sees my mother, hides behind
the legs of her own mother and whispers,
"She's an Indian and she has a braid."

These strands stretch on forever.
I see them creeping into my uncle's
beer cans, twisting themselves
through IVs at the local hospital
where a young brown man
waits for protease inhibitors
His grandmother is singing
>*Giga Giga*
>*Anhdadi'a*
>*(Blood Blood*
>*Remember).*

When I get home Jackson's hands
are rubbing together with the crack
of kindling. He is thinking of so much
more. He is writing a New Age book.
He is making a dream catcher.
He is mining minerals from the Black Hills.
He is leaving trails across the continent.

# Mutiny

Tomorrow I could be found
covered in blood
acrid syrup that lures
bees and butterflies in
frenzied swarms
My shroud
alive and humming

The skinhead on the corner
stands righteous
black boots
threaded with white laces
He longs to see my throat

I know how to vanish
into shadows dodge bullets
cops
      cocks
            jocks
slip though front lines
remain unsliced and whole

A friend who does not know
these things gives advice
*You should get out more*
*Not live so much*
*in words*

But this is target practice
Mutiny
Sharpening phrases into razors

I will surround myself with sunflowers
wrap the milky way
around my shoulders
seek lovers
whose scent is survival

I will build an arsenal
stockpile words
tie poems to firebombs

Burn this mess down

## Song of Removal

Big Mountain chanting New Echota
Wounded Knee chanting Tellico
Peabody Western Coal burning Diné
University of British Colombia poisoning Gros Ventre
Broken Hill Propriety Co. Ltd. wearing bones on wedding rings
Joined forever with death
And we are still being removed

And this white girl who lives on the stolen lands of the Southern
        Ute and the Diné says *People on the east coast think we're still*
        *fighting the Indians*
As if their ranch homes are not built on burial mounds
As if we are not still being removed

And 1838 chants 1996
and 1492 chants 2003
and Bush chants Jackson
and we are still being removed

And I hear white folks say
*I didn't kill the Indians*
*Didn't put them on reservations*
*Why should I be responsible*
not seeing that when the government
wants our land they
remove us
remove us
remove us
remove us

and if we resist we are killed
and reservations are death camps

and Arizona chants Ontario
and Oaxaca chants Tahlequah
and San Francisco chants Cape Town
and we are still being removed

In Denver walk by Indians
Old men sitting on concrete
sitting on bones
sitting in a circle
passing beer in a circle
listening to sacred chants on a portable radio in a circle
dying in a circle

and Budweiser chants Columbus
and AIDS chants smallpox
and senators chant murderers
and we are still being removed

And this white college student says to me
*I hate it when Hispanics won't speak English*
*This is our country*

But it is not your country
Never will be your country
and the Xicano and the Xicana
shall speak whatever they choose
shall keep alive their ancestors
shall keep living
and I wonder why you don't speak Cheyenne

And while Disney paints Pocahontas the great white wet dream
while Russell Means sells out
military occupation of our homes persists
We are still being removed

And we shall be removed
and shall resist
and they shall kill us
but we shall not die

and our tongues shall be stolen
but we shall take them back
and we shall lift our elders off the concrete
and they shall weep in our arms
and we shall weep with them
and we shall stomp on concrete
and it shall crumble

and we shall drum on monuments
and monuments shall fall
and we shall find the bones of our people
and bones shall dance

and in the North borders shall vanish
and in the South borders shall vanish
and in the East oceans shall rejoice
and in the West oceans shall rejoice

and they shall remove us no more
but we shall always remember

we shall sing of removals
we shall sing of removals
we shall sing of removals
we shall sing of removals

and the Ancestors shall sing
and the People shall sing
and the Animals shall sing
and the Earth shall sing

and mothers chant children
and fathers chant children
and Sun chants Moon
and Sky chants Earth

and we are still being removed

## Back to the Blanket

I am learning to take each body part back,
rebeautify the space between our skin, unknit the shadows
that still loom like vengeful gods in memory's doorway.

Here, we are out of reach from their hands dripping
with gold from our hills. They locked us in, away, cut our hair,
    burned
our tongues until they were covered with landscapes of scars.

We were forced to kneel before men who were not God, told to
    work
that we might be saved from a cursed destiny made manifest
    with each breath.
They prayed for the starvation of songs created between our
    skins.

Come here. Let me kiss your wounds away, the mark
on your back a rigid angle of conquest.

Your body does not smell like candles or scrubbing powder
or centuries of terror we could not lock out.

We go back to the blanket. You grasp my hips, handfuls of earth,
my heart softened by the rub of your hands.

Let me wrap you in ceremony, a giveaway of straining muscle,
    the soft whispered
stories of our flesh. Let me suck the sickness out with this old-
    time medicine.

Make love to me until I forget their stale language.
From your feet on up you are beautiful. You weave splendor with
    simple tools.

Feed me the traditions your body would not forget.

# Story

Sometimes the boy imagines his hair flows in thick crests around his body. He can see it blow behind him as it whips the air. He can hear it as it cracks the sound barrier. He can smell it spark around his head, electricity zapping the dry, fierce winter. Sometimes he imagines his hair roots itself in the ground, dislodges soil, searches for water and minerals in the dense beige clay of the prairie. He sees himself as a tree. He sees himself turn all his leaves toward heaven to soak up light and warmth. The boy wonders if trees are as cold as he is at 2:30 A.M. as he exits his friend's car and walks towards his front door. "FAGGOTT!" The word hits the ground, bounces into the gutter and rattles itself across the chilled pavement like a discarded peach pit. It lands near the toe of his left boot and stares up at him. For a moment his feet stick to the sidewalk. He turns around to find out where the word was thrown from. In the shadows of branches stand two men, immovable. They do not flinch, they watch. He wonders how long they have been there, waiting in the dark. They must have sprouted out of the gravel and oil of the dusty parking lot, warmed by the pink fire of streetlights. "FUCKING BITCH!" The words hit him like hail. He hurries up the stairs to his apartment, unlocks the door with the dull jingle of keys, slips inside and locks the door with his right hand at the same moment his left hand switches off the living room light. Wooden floorboards groaning under his panicked steps, he turns off all the lights. Inside his chest his heart has turned into a bird ensnared in barbed wire, its yellow feathers tipped in crimson as it tries to break free. His heart flails behind his ribcage. It will not be able to get out. It is already home. The boy comforts his heart as he peers carefully out the window. The men are gone, as if blown away by a storm.

Sometimes the boy imagines he has wings and can fly like Gabriel, like an angel in golden robes. He can feel his hair as it cascades behind him. He can feel air as it pushes through wine colored feathers. He can fly so high that not one limb of the highest tree can ensnare him. He imagines the change in atmosphere as he hurries to a place where he is warm. The boy looks out into the chilled streets. He stands near the window as if he has taken root in the worn planks of his floor. He touches the icy white walls of his shadowed apartment with his fingertips. He is already home.

# Night Terrors

The hair brush falls to the floor
and he starts to cry
trembling terror in his sleep
I stay awake
hold him tight
tight
tight
So he doesn't fall
doesn't float away
Knowing about the rape I'm sure he will
Being raped by a friend is already too much
but then he tells me
*I never feel safe at night*
*My father used to come into my room and use me as a punching bag*


I was 14 when I was eaten by the monster with the ice blue eyes
After that
After he spit me out
After that he would find me when I ate lunch
*Did you have fun last night*
drive up and down my neighborhood
warning
Don't ever tell
And I didn't
Soon dreams of the man in my house
in my room
the blood of my parents and sisters on the fake white wood
        paneling
everything dark and sticky

Coming after me next
I stopped dreaming

*I leave my body when it happens now* she said
*I float away*
You would have to
surviving rape from your father
while your sister is forced to watch
these customary night murders
and the countless other rapes from other men
would make you float away
not able to scream or kick
Those burnt almond eyes have seen too much
Soon you learn to float

After the dreams stopped the night terrors began
The sudden bloodglass that strikes me as I sleep
Can't wake up
scream
move
Sometimes I float
I leave my body in my bed to search for help
traveling like wind
Wailing spirit
*Wake me up Wake me up*
*Wake me up Wake me up*
*Somebody*
*Somebody help me*
I haven't had a nightmare in years
This is something else
Can't explain floating to someone who doesn't have to

*Ring around the rosies*
*a pocket full of posies*
*ashes ashes*
*we all fall down*

She keeps her closet door open at all times
The fear that daddy will jump out again and rape her more
We still wonder how he knew the rest of the family was out of
     the house
How he knew each time she was alone
How he knew when to leave his jeering notes
*Daddy loves his little girl*
*See you soon*

We are screaming
but no one will hear us
We are trying to wake up from
this terror
but cannot
Millions of eyes shut tight
tight
tight
when we walk by
Sometimes
Sometimes we float

His baby sitter raped him
Every night after dinner the creature would say
*I need you to help me with something*
*Can't someone else help you this time?*
hoping more than anything he could float away
He would vomit afterwards
The clorox smell of cum
mixed with stomach acid
splashing in the upstairs toilet

Even when it's over
it is not
Even when it's over there are terrors in the night
When it's over
we learn how to float

*Children weep and children sleep*
*and children keep their secrets*

*America* a voice is calling to you from the woods
*America* a voice is calling to you from the streets
*America* a voice is calling to you from your closets

Be warned
America
there are monsters in your homes
that do more than just go bump in the night

# Two Approaches to Memory

I.

Sge, Memory! You are weak!
Ni! Your paths are black!
I am a ballplayer
covered in bear grease
and slip from your feeble hands!

Sge, Memory! You are weak!
Ni! Your paths are black!
The White Spider
crawls across her web
to swallow your puny corpse!

Sge, Memory! You are weak!
Ni! Your paths are black!
You cannot catch me!
I am a swift deer
your arrows never pierce!

Sge, Memory! You are weak!
Ni! Your paths are black!
The White Rattlesnake
slithers towards you
to strike your ugly face!

Ha!

II.

O, Memory,
You sweet,
heartbroken thing.

Tonight I hold
my genitals softly
in callused palm,
whisper your name.

O, Memory,
You precious,
trembling thing.


Tonight I forgive you.
You, inviolable
and innocent as
my aching skin.

O, Memory,
You holy,
broken thing.

Come back to me.

I am ready now
to hold you
as my own.

## I Want to Bite Words

See them spilling
from your mouth
like corn seeds
Plant rows
in the forbidden crackle
between the envelopes
of our flesh
Touch the wheat
of your cheek and
braid it into
possibilities and
the irresistibility
                    of stars

Your words
are grain
I must sew
and harvest

Your fingers
dripping syllables
I piece together
like a quilt

If I can create
a place for you
between thumb
and index finger
in the forbidden crackle
between pen
and paper surely
you can create
a place for me
between teeth
and tongue between

right arm
and left between
arms and chest
rising and falling
with the imperceptibility
of spirit between
inhalations
of breath and the vibrations
of skin in throat

I am not printing
these words across
my skin for them
to be ignored
I am not balancing
vowels on my chest
for them to be
mispronounced
I leave them there
for you to devour
roundness until
we are dizzy
and irresistible
in the swollen air

Taste my meanings
on the curve of my arms
in the spice of my sweat
I touch you where the water
of your hair meets
the earth of your neck
I kiss your spine like
sun warming

silk wrap
discoveries around
my fingers touch
your lips
your tongue
your teeth sharp
with mystery that dares
                    to bite

# Book of Memory
*for all victims of hate crimes, and for those of us who survive*

What prayers will save us

Here at the genesis of
a terrified century
there is work to do

We construct words from
shrapnel and despair
fasten them with images of the missing
sculpt anguish into seismic rebellion

We shudder under
the weight of loss
fall to our knees before
the rubble of our dead

Look at the frantic geometries
we once named Bill, Tyra, Hattie Mae, Michelle
The jutting fractures we once named
Mother, Lover, Sister, Son

What can I offer
but these turbulent tears
my heart broken into
infinite shapes of sorrow

Write it in a book of memory
that as the powerful laugh
at our earth shattering loss
we the merciful
gather like whirlwinds of fire
embrace each other
in mourning and rage
wipe tears from each other's cheeks
and whisper

*There is work to be done*

We fall before the voices
left in hate's wake
and open a book of memory
to record improvisations of spirit
revolutions of flesh
our mutinous love

Here
at the genesis of a dangerous millennium
we intone names against fists and bullets

Here
before this splintered destruction
we gently open earth
gather the pieces left
to quilt a new story

As our dead watch and wait
we become
the prayers
that save us

## Miracle, For Colin

What impossible
n sweet          dark       chocolate
the resistance  of your breath

# At the Queer Conference Dinner

I looked into your dark eyes
with shock
when you asked me if I could
do a traditional Indian dance
to entertain these mostly
white faces
All these white faces
except yours and
a few others I could count
on one hand
and I spit out the word
NO
like a rock
hoping its sound falling
to the floor would wake
you up from all these lies
they've fed us
It didn't
I left the room
to stand in the parking
lot and smoke

Brother
How angry I was
for being angry with you
Your young Azteca body
shrouded in the expensive
business clothes
white men wear when they
write out contracts to
sell our grandmothers' hearts
I know you are pleading only
to stay alive
and

One day I will
dance for you
It will be my prayer
that you come home

# Blessing

On the wind of my
breath I send you blessings.

I send you strength. Seven!
I send you patience. Seven!
I send you love. Seven!
I send you honesty. Seven!

Grandmother Spider weaves you
a white web to keep you
away from the Nightland. Four!

In the blood of fear is
the life of the Mother. Four!

All birds give you lessons
of strength. Four!

Your paths are white.
They offer you gifts. Four!

You will walk to the
East. Your ancestors
praise you and hold
you upright. Four!

I send my blessings on
my breath.

# A Long Story Made Short

So I'm home alone at midnight
and there is this "ding-dong" at my door
and it's this guy I know and he's drunk as usual
and with his buddy and I think
    *Fuck*
    *I just wanted to make my fry bread*

So this ding-donger walks into my home like he owns it
(in typical colonist fashion)
and starts looking at one of my Native magazines and he says
    *Why do you have this You're not aboriginal*
and I say
    *Yes I am*
and he says
    *No you're not*
and I'm in no mood to discuss my racial/cultural heritages with
    a ding-donger so I say
    *Yes*
    *I am*
and leave it at that adding more flour to my fry bread which is
    too thin and sticky

So then the ding- donger decides to bring up a feminist bumper
    sicker on my friend's car
and he tries to claim it's sexist
    *How do you deduce that*
I ask and he says it's narrow and that it means all straight white
    men are assholes
blah
        blah
                blah

I want to add rich and able-bodied
but instead I say
      *You're drowning in white male guilt*
but Ding-Donger says he isn't so I plop my fry bread down on a cookie
      sheet and start kneading the sloppy bread pretending it's this
      man's pasty face

Ding-Donger is blitzed out of his head and is touching me way too
      much which pisses me off because
      one: I didn't invite him to
      two: He's straight (or says he is)
and I think
      *What makes you think you can touch me just because I'm a Faggot and*
      *cooking fry bread and in a skirt*

and yes indeedy sexism is the root of homophobia
because somehow this ding-donger thinks because
I'm a fairy (Not really a man) At least not like him (Thank God)
I won't take this sticky ball of water and flour and smear it on his face

Too bad I haven't started heating up the oil
so I could fry up his hand until it bubbles golden brown
in this iron pan and I could eat it with some beans
or maybe honey
which seems to be this guy's favorite
since he keeps calling me that like I've got a label on my container
      reading
"Lucky Clover"

And when he comes up behind me and puts his arms around my waist
and kisses me on the cheek and neck like I'm some kind of bread that
needs a crust I wish
I had a fine-toothed comb
to rake down his face and then
maybe add some of his blood to my mix

cuz as a faggot
I'd like my fry bread pink

But he leaves for more beer
and I'm grateful he's an alcoholic so he has a motivation (ding-donger
    though it is) to get out of my house
He leaves his hat
which makes me nervous cuz I don't want him to come back for it

So I leave my bread to rise and wash the dough off my hands
but the anger doesn't come off
and stains my fingers
and clothes

So I take a piece of paper
and smear the anger into a sign
which reads:
    *The mixed faggot's makin' fry bread*
    *No ding-dongers allowed*

# Legacy
*for my Osage grandmothers*

The weeping face of
the woman in the brown dress
roars in my memory

She holds her legs apart
her skirt a basket
filled with guns and men's voices
It's all that is left
That and a book she fills
with papers    money   BIA cards
Soon she will burn it too

The clouds look like loaves of bread
and none of us can reach them

We stuff our bellies with soil
Pray for wings

# Chantway for FC

I.

From the heavy debris of loss
we emerge
with giveaways of yellow and white corn
to anoint the tip of your tongue
feast on the memory of your first laughter
sing an honor song
to the slow heart beat
of your final breaths

Together we emerge
 voices strained and weary from wailing

We emerge in beauty
You will be our song

II.

Grief pulls me
down canyon walls

*There I wander*

to search for imprints
your hands left in dust

*There I wander*

Hold up hot fierce
blueness of Colorado sky

*There I wander*

Listen for your breath
caught in branches

*There I wander*

Hunger for your voice
in a pinion jay's throat

*There I return*

Your spirit fingers push us
to incant witness to your body
Feet pointed east
where sun stains sky
crimson and gold
Hands cradling your precious
brown belly
Hair pulled into a ponytail
like a river of obsidian

Our muscles arc rainbows
Spiral galaxies around you
Rock your lost flesh
Bare you up open palmed
Sacred

III.

Our homelands grow fertile
from our blood
sprout abundance
Feed multitudes
while we daily count our disappeared

What is breath
if it cannot hurl storms across the continent

What are words
that can't block blows
shade you from sun's white light
like large merciful wings
Drop cool sweet water
into your mouth
Stop blood's flow into dust

We count preciousness daily
Hold you as warriors
brothers
sisters
Hold you
with words and breath

Rise
in beauty

IV.

The shocking whirl
of your hair and fingerprints
mimics wind that gives us breath

You are the rustle of leaves
whirlwinds of dust
feathered smoke rising from sage

We will sew you a gown of white shells
threaded with yellow zigzag lightning

Adorn you with black clouds
brush blue corn pollen across your lips
braid thunder through your hair

We will be your breath
We will be your song

V.

It is finished in beauty
It is finished in beauty

*In memoriam: FC Martinez, Jr.*

CPSIA information can be obtained
at www.ICGtesting.com
Printed in the USA
LVHW03s1854230718
584651LV00003B/657/P